EXPLORE AI

BRAINY COMPUTERS

SONYA NEWLAND

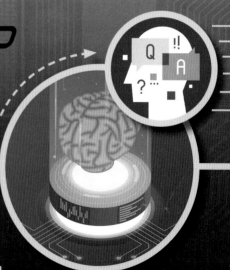

WAYLAND
www.waylandbooks.co.uk

First published in Great Britain in 2021 by Wayland

Copyright © Hodder & Stoughton Limited, 2021

Produced for Wayland by
White-Thomson Publishing Ltd
www.wtpub.co.uk

Editor: Sonya Newland
Designer: Dan Prescott, Couper Street Type Co.

HB ISBN: 978 1 5263 1486 4
PB ISBN: 978 1 5263 1487 1
10 9 8 7 6 5 4 3 2 1

MIX
Paper from
responsible sources
FSC® C104740

Wayland
An imprint of Hachette Children's Group
Part of Hodder & Stoughton
Carmelite House
50 Victoria Embankment
London EC4Y 0DZ

An Hachette UK Company
www.hachette.co.uk
www.hachettechildrens.co.uk

Printed in Dubai

You can find words in **bold**
in the glossary on page 30.

The publisher would like to thank the following for permission to reproduce their pictures:
Alamy: Rowan Morgan 25m; Getty Images: Stan Honda/AFP 12, Ben Hider 13m; Shutterstock: Julia
Rada 4, 1000s_pixels 5t, goodluz 5l, Gorodenkoff 5m, New Africa 5r, Visual Generation 6t, VVadyab
Pico 6bl, Graphite and Charcoal 6br, EQRoy 7t, mayrum 7bl, denvitruk 7br, Ryzhi 8, CobraCZ 9t,
ShadeDesign 9b, BestfForBest 10t, Media Guru 10bl, AlenaK 10br, vasabii 11t, Vitalii Petrenko 11b,
siridhata 13t, Good Studio 13t, Vector Up 13b, Blamb 14t, cosmaa 14b, chaipanya 15t, Blablo101 15b,
Wor Sang Jun 16l, Inspiring 16r, Makhnach_S 17, VLADGRIN 18, Dzianis_Rakhuba 19t, Ranta Images
19b, ElenVD 20t, Taleseedum 20t, 21t, Batshevs 20b, Oleksandr Panasovskyi 21t, Pavlo Plakhotia
21b, metamorworks 22t, Guy Erwood 22b, Zyabich 23t, Visual Generation 23b, VectorMine 24t,
Nadia Snopek 24b, Vectorfair.com 25t, Jane Kelly 25b, 26t, fizkes 26b, metrue 27l, Petr Pohudka 27r,
vladwel 28, denvitruk 29t, Lemberg Vector studio 29b.

All design elements from Shutterstock.

Every effort has been made to clear copyright. Should there be any inadvertent omission,
please apply to the publisher for rectification.

The website addresses (URLs) included in this book were valid at the time of going to press.
However, it is possible that contents or addresses may have changed since the publication of this
book. No responsibility for any such changes can be accepted by either the author or the publisher.

CONTENTS

WHAT IS AI?

Artificial Intelligence (AI) is the science, technology and engineering of intelligent machines. AI is all around you – a part of your everyday life. A lot of the time you might not even realise that the devices you interact with are 'intelligent'!

AMAZING AI ABILITIES

The goal of AI is to create machines that use human-like intelligence to perform many different tasks. These might be practical jobs, such as mowing the lawn. But they may also be incredibly tricky tasks where the machine has to think and learn.

HUMANS – THE ULTIMATE MACHINES

Your brain is an amazing machine, carrying out complex processes every second of every day. It's how you think, feel, react, reason, analyse, learn and explain. Understanding human abilities like these is key to AI – recreating these processes in machines is what makes artificial intelligence so 'real'.

AI uses ideas from many different scientific fields, including: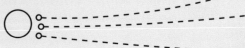

WHAT ARE INTELLIGENT COMPUTERS?

Ordinary computers seem pretty smart, don't they? But everything they do is the result of a clever human programming them that way. Intelligent computers are a bit different. Using AI technology, they can 'see' and 'hear'. They can plan, learn and solve problems like you can. Sometimes AI computers can do things even better than humans!

WHERE WILL IT LEAD?

As computers get smarter, some people have started to question whether intelligent technology is a good thing. What if we come to rely on machines too much? What if computers become so like humans that they start to make mistakes, just like we do? AI engineers consider **ethical** questions carefully in their work.

computer science

neuroscience

psychology

5

CAN MACHINES THINK?

It's easy enough to test an ordinary machine – you just set it running and see if it does the job it was designed to do. But early AI engineers faced a bigger challenge. How would they know for sure that a computer was intelligent? One man came up with an ingenious way to measure machine intelligence.

THE TURING TEST

In 1950, British mathematician Alan Turing published an important paper. It began with the question 'Can machines think?' Turing invented a kind of game to see whether a computer was clever enough to fool a person into thinking it was human.

PLAYER C (HUMAN TESTER)

The 'tester' asks Player A and Player B questions. The tester doesn't know which player is the human and which is the computer – they have to work it out from the responses. If the computer fools the tester into thinking it's human, it has passed the test.

PLAYER A (COMPUTER)

The computer doesn't have to get the answers right. The real test of its intelligence is whether it can respond in the same way that a human would.

PLAYER B (HUMAN)

The human player simply answers the questions.

BRIGHT MINDS

Alan Turing (1912–54) was a brilliant mathematician and computer scientist. During the Second World War (1939–45), he designed an incredible code-breaking machine that helped Britain and its allies win the war. After the war, Turing went to work at the University of Manchester, where he helped to build the first working digital computer.

Throughout the war, more than 200 Turing–Welchman 'Bombe' machines were built to break the code the Germans used to keep their war plans secret.

EUGENE GOOSTMAN

For decades, no computer managed to pass the test. Then, in 2014, along came Eugene Goostman. Some people believe that this **chatbot** was the first computer to win Turing's 'imitation game'. In a series of tests, Eugene Goostman convinced 33 per cent of its testers that it was human.

Some people claim that Google Duplex was really the first computer program to pass the Turing Test. This artificial intelligence has a voice just like a real person. To put it to the test, Duplex's creators had it call up a hairdressing salon. The person who answered the call booked an appointment without ever suspecting they were talking to a computer!

AI
IN ACTION

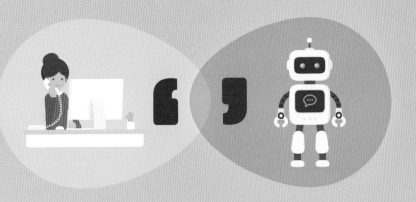

EARLY AI IDEAS

By the 1950s, there was a big buzz about artificial intelligence. Everyone was interested in what people might be able to do with intelligent machines. But the leading scientists of the time disagreed on how AI should be applied.

TOP-DOWN...

Some experts felt that that AI needed a 'top-down' approach. This meant programming computers with the 'rules' of human behaviour, such as how to feel or react in particular situations. If a computer knew these rules, it would be able to respond intelligently to tasks.

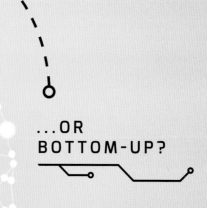

...OR BOTTOM-UP?

Others argued that computers should be built with **neural networks**, a bit like human brain cells, or **neurons**. In this way, a computer would be able to 'learn' new behaviours by itself. This became known as the 'bottom-up' approach.

```
(lambda (s1 s2 . pred?)
    (let (((<= (if (null? pred?) <= (car pred?))
        (let merge ((s1 s1)
                    (s2 s2))
```

 John McCarthy (1927–2011) was an American **cognitive scientist** who was known as the 'father of AI'. In fact, it was McCarthy who first used the term 'artificial intelligence', in 1955. He invented an AI programming language called Lisp, which is still used in AI technology today.

Lisp stands for LISt Processing. It is one of the longest-lived computer languages ever created.

THE 'AI WINTER'

By the 1970s, AI scientists had little to show for all their big plans. People invested less money in creating this new technology, and the public started to lose interest in the idea. This period was later called the 'AI winter'.

WINTER TO SPRING

But in the early 1980s, everything changed. Some experts suggested ways that artificial intelligence could be used to make money – and that got people interested again! Instead of trying to develop machines with a broad general intelligence, AI engineers decided to focus on particular tasks. AI had a new direction.

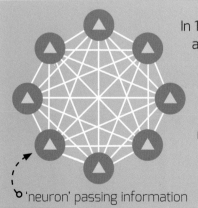

'neuron' passing information

In 1982, a physicist called John Hopfield created an artificial neural network. The Hopfield Network could store and recall information like the human brain. The 'neurons' were either on or off, and they switched depending on information they received from other 'neurons'. The network could store a number of different patterns or memories.

AI
IN ACTION

WEAK AND STRONG

Experts divide AI into two main types – weak and strong. Each type has different functions and uses.

WEAK AI

Weak AI is technology that has been designed to perform one particular task really well. In weak AI, the computer is not truly 'intelligent', it just behaves as if it was. It mimics intelligence through a set of programmed rules.

STRONG AI

Strong AI is when a computer can reason, think, learn and perform tasks on its own. Some strong AI is human-like – the computer's behaviour and **reasoning** are similar to ours. In non-human strong AI, the computer evolves its own way of thinking and reasoning.

At the moment, most AI is weak AI. For example, personal assistant systems like Siri are designed to do one specific job.

Strong AI can tackle an unfamiliar task by thinking for itself and working out how to do it.

Weak AI can get better at the task it's been designed for, but it can't learn new tasks.

HUMAN ABILITIES

Weak and strong AI both aim to recreate important human abilities and processes in machines.

KNOWLEDGE: storing and retrieving information

REASONING: thinking about things in a logical way

PROBLEM-SOLVING: finding solutions to difficult issues

PERCEPTION: using the senses to see, hear or become aware of things

PLANNING: thinking ahead to map out how to do something

LEARNING: acquiring new knowledge and skills through study or experience

Super AI is even stronger than strong AI – machines that are more intelligent than humans. No super AI exists at the moment, but machines may one day be better than us at everything, from maths to sports!

BRAIN BIOLOGY

Part of the problem in the early years of AI was that there was still a lot that scientists didn't know about the way these human processes worked. In the 1990s, developments in neuroscience helped experts understand how different parts of the brain worked in much more detail, which gave them a better idea of how to develop AI.

WHAT IF...? What if scientists create a machine that has its own form of intelligence, with different ways of thinking and reasoning to us? What benefits could there be to discovering new ways of thinking? What dangers might there be?

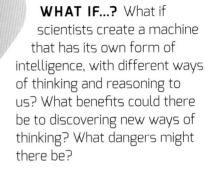

FANCY A GAME?

Game-playing computers were among the earliest intelligent machines. They are a good example of AI's top-down approach (see page 8), as they are programmed with a set of rules.

DEEP BLUE

In 1995, the computer company IBM revealed a chess-playing computer called Deep Blue. It had been programmed to understand the rules of the game chess, and could analyse millions of different positions on the board. The big question was: could it think strategically? That is, could it plan ahead and anticipate what its opponent might do?

World chess champion Garry Kasparov took up the Deep Blue challenge. They drew three games, Kasparov won one game and Deep Blue won two. This was the first time a computer beat a human.

Intelligent computer Deep Blue beats chess champion Garry Kasparov in May 1997.

. d4 d5 3. Nc3 dxe4

IBM WATSON

Jeopardy! is a TV quiz show with a difference. Contestants are given clues as statements, and they have to phrase their answer as a question.

Riddle-like questions are very difficult for a computer brain to understand. The computer IBM Watson had years of training to recognise patterns in questions and answers. When put to the test, AI won the day. IBM Watson beat the two top contestants the show had ever had.

QUESTION:
This supercomputer beat chess champ Garry Kasparov in 1997.

ANSWER:
What is Deep Blue?

IBM Watson takes on a human *Jeopardy!* contestant.

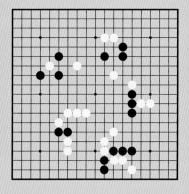

AlphaGo is a computer program that plays the ancient Chinese board game Go. The rules of Go are simple, but there are trillions of possible positions on the board. Human players trust their **intuition**, but that's something computers can't do. Despite that, in 2016, AlphaGo used its amazing neural network to beat the best Go player in the world, Lee Sedol.

AI
IN ACTION

DECISION-MAKING

HUMANS...

Problem-solving and decision-making are important human skills. We use them for many different reasons: when playing games, working out how to get somewhere – even when deciding what to have for breakfast! We use processes such as reasoning, learning and **recall** to make decisions in different ways.

A lot of decision-making is unconscious. Choosing the same cereal for breakfast is a habit-based decision. It happens in a deep part of the brain called the basal ganglia.

Habit-based problem-solving is often a matter of **instinct** – we 'trust our gut' and let the emotional part of our brain find the answer for us.

Some decisions are based on information we receive. Value-based decisions are ones that we make after considering this information.

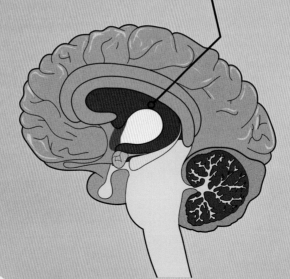

Value-based decisions are made more slowly than habit-based ones. When making them, we tend to follow 'rules' that we have been told or that we remember.

Humans can take advantage of their opponent's mistakes. But they also have a basic instinct to cooperate with each other.

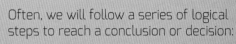

Often, we will follow a series of logical steps to reach a conclusion or decision:

- Identify the question or problem.
- Weigh up the information.
- Consider the different solutions.
- Pick the best solution.
- Carry out the solution.

...VS. MACHINES

You can think of an algorithm as a kind of flowchart. It contains a set of instructions, represented by symbols. Instructions are carried out in a certain order.

Computers make decisions based on patterns in the data they receive. They use **algorithms** to solve problems in the same way that humans use steps. Algorithms can work out thousands of different outcomes in seconds, then choose the best one.

The 'decision' may be 'yes' or 'no'. The following instructions might take the form of:
IF [...] THEN [...]
ELSE [...]

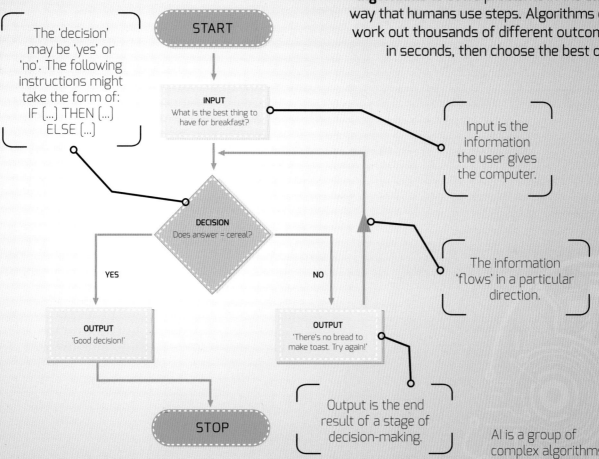

START

INPUT
What is the best thing to have for breakfast?

Input is the information the user gives the computer.

DECISION
Does answer = cereal?

YES

NO

The information 'flows' in a particular direction.

OUTPUT
'Good decision!'

OUTPUT
'There's no bread to make toast. Try again!'

Output is the end result of a stage of decision-making.

STOP

AI is a group of complex algorithms that can modify its algorithms and even create new ones to improve the decision-making process.

Computers don't have instincts like humans do, which probably gives them an advantage in games!

EXPERTS AT EVERYTHING

An 'expert system' is a special type of AI. It is a computer system that can work things out (reason) and make decisions about a specific area of knowledge, in the same way that a human expert can.

TRUE OR FALSE?

Expert systems are based on logic. For example, if you flip a coin you know that, logically, it will land on either heads or tails. In computing, a system called Boolean logic works on the same idea. In a Boolean system, data is represented as one of two values: true or false.

Start with a statement that is true or false:

It is daytime.

From this you can form other statements that are either true or false using **fundamental operators** (AND, OR, NOT) to continue the logic.

It is daytime. AND It is Tuesday.

This helps the computer understand the task. For example, if your smart home computer is programmed to turn on the lights at night on Saturdays, it won't turn them on during the day on a Tuesday!

FUZZY LOGIC

But not everything is as black and white as Boolean logic suggests. That's where 'fuzzy logic' comes in. Fuzzy logic deals with partial truth and probabilities.

Expert systems based on fuzzy logic are very important in helping intelligent computers understand things like language.

BOOLEAN LOGIC

Is it hot outside?	
Yes	No

FUZZY LOGIC

Is it hot outside?			
Extremely hot	Very hot	A bit hot	Less than a bit hot

WHAT IF...? Computers that can make their own decisions seem like a great idea. But what if a computer is deciding whether a flight should be cancelled because of bad weather? Or whether a prisoner should be released? What factors might a machine *not* consider that a human would?

Created in 1978, R1/XCON was one of the first examples of an expert system. It was designed to help customers who were ordering computer systems. It used artificial intelligence to work out all the different pieces of **hardware** and **software** required to build the right computer system for a particular customer's needs.

AI
IN ACTION

WHAT DID YOU SAY?

Without language, how could we learn? How would we say what we want or how we feel? Communication is a big part of our lives. And AI is helping to break down language barriers.

BEYOND BINARY

If you don't know a word, you look it up in a dictionary or figure it out by its context. Researchers are creating AI algorithms so computers can do the same. They will find the word in an online dictionary or guess what it means from the words around it.

When you think of computers and language, you probably think of **binary code** or a programming language like Java. But AI engineers are working on ways to teach computers to understand human languages too.

WHAT IF...? What if AI allows us all to speak any language we like at the touch of a button? Will understanding each other more fully make the world a better place? What skills might be gained by such technology? And what skills might be lost?

SPEAKING OTHER LANGUAGES

How great would it be if you could speak another language without having to sit through lessons? Now you can, thanks to some amazing AI technology. For example, Skype now lets you talk to foreign friends in their own language.

Skype Translator can translate speech in real time into 10 different languages.

THE TROUBLE WITH LANGUAGE

Natural language processing (NLP) is an AI process that helps computers overcome some human language problems:

INTENT: Everyone expresses things differently. NLP helps computers work out *meaning* (intent) in the user's words.

WORD BOUNDARIES: When you speak, do you leave a gap between words? Most of us don't! Why might that make spoken words hard for a computer to understand?

SPELLING, GRAMMAR AND PUNCTUATION: NLP technology can fix things like spelling mistakes. It also understands grammatical structures.

When you hear someone speak you don't just hear their words, you also interpret them – you work out what they mean.

AI
IN ACTION

Many people flee their own countries because of war or poverty. When they arrive in a new country, they often can't speak the language. This makes it hard for them to get the help they need. Capiche is an amazing piece of AI designed for refugees. It can translate speech from one language to another. It also checks legal documents – and can even identify fake news!

LANGUAGE

HUMANS...

Every time you hear or read words, the language centres in the brain kick into action. They make sense of the words you hear. They also allow you to respond using words of your own.

UNDERSTANDING: Wernicke's area is in the temporal lobe. It helps humans to *understand* speech and language.

SPEAKING: Broca's area is in the frontal lobe. This is the part of the brain that helps humans to *produce* speech and language.

HEARING: The brain registers the sound of words in the auditory cortex. This is where the process begins.

INTERPRETING: The ventral stream helps us identify what someone is saying (content) and interpret it (understanding).

REPRODUCING: The dorsal stream helps us to reproduce the same speech. patterns.

Thanks to these processes...

...we can talk to each other!

...VS. MACHINES

REASONING: Even if users don't express themselves clearly, the chatbot can work out what they mean. This makes the conversation sound natural.

INTERACTION: By interacting with the user, the chatbot learns what they need (intent) so it can find a solution.

Chatbots are a type of AI software. They are programmed to imitate some human processes. That means they can have a real-time conversation with a human user over a computer.

LEARNING: Over time, the chatbot learns from corrections users make. This improves its responses.

MEMORY: The chatbot can remember what was said earlier in a conversation – or even things that were said in a different conversation.

UNDERSTANDING: A chatbot doesn't just choose from a range of standard replies. It reads text in human languages and even understands sentence structures.

Thanks to these processes...

...we can understand each other!

WHAT CAN YOU SEE?

In the early days of AI, scientists thought they could teach computers to 'see' in a similar way to how human vision works. They soon realised that this process was too difficult to copy – but the solution they came up with for computer vision sometimes gives even better results!

FACIAL RECOGNITION

You've probably seen facial recognition in action – many social media apps use it. Every time you tag a friend, you're helping to improve the app's AI! Your computer may also be able to organise your photos by recognising people's faces.

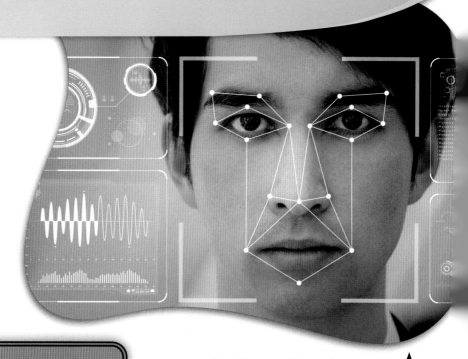

Humans are better than computers at some things. We could recognise that this was a statue of Alan Turing, but even an intelligent computer that had 'seen' a photo of Turing probably wouldn't make the connection.

Facial recognition software can identify the unique features of someone's face. This is similar to the way that fingerprint identification works – every person is different.

Computers can distinguish features more precisely than humans. For example, some AI can identify different but very similar breeds of dogs, which humans would find hard to tell apart!

Snapchat is famous for the stickers and visual effects you can add to your photos, allowing you to manipulate images to make funny faces. To do this, the app uses digital **nodes** to map out facial features. Once the software has this map, it can adapt the image.

AI
IN ACTION

OPEN YOUR EYES

Eye-gaze is AI technology that allows the user to control a computer with just their eyes. You can scroll down a page by moving your eyes and click by blinking. This technology could open up a whole new world for people who are paralysed. It may also help doctors diagnose diseases such as Alzheimer's.

A group of researchers wanted to see if they could fool facial recognition software. They digitally added a pair of fancy patterned glasses to someone's photo to see if it prevented the software from identifying that person. It worked!

VISUAL PERCEPTION

HUMANS...

Visual perception refers to how we see things – and how we interpret what we see. Experts still don't fully understand how the human brain interprets images. But they do know how our brain *receives* images.

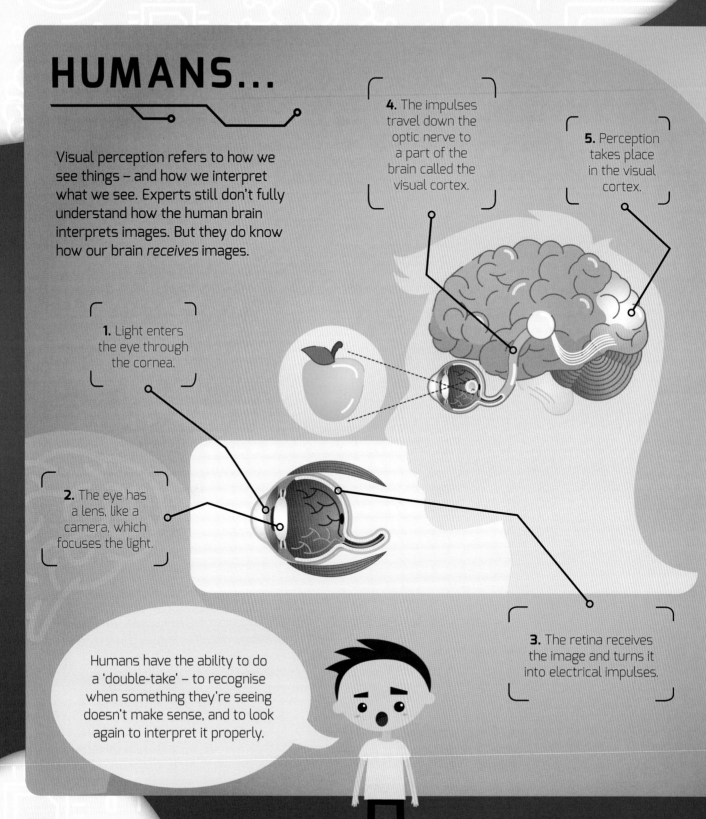

4. The impulses travel down the optic nerve to a part of the brain called the visual cortex.

5. Perception takes place in the visual cortex.

1. Light enters the eye through the cornea.

2. The eye has a lens, like a camera, which focuses the light.

3. The retina receives the image and turns it into electrical impulses.

Humans have the ability to do a 'double-take' – to recognise when something they're seeing doesn't make sense, and to look again to interpret it properly.

...VS. MACHINES

1. The computer's camera captures images.

2. The computer detects the pixels that make up the image.

Computers see things differently. Their 'eyes' are built-in cameras, which receive images from the outside world. The computer interprets those images by recognising patterns in **pixels**.

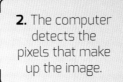

3. It then finds the edges of the image to get a more specific shape.

4. After that it can detect the contours of the subject to identify differences in shapes, colours and textures.

5. It then detects the whole object to identify what it is 'seeing'.

Computers may interpret an image incorrectly, but they won't realise that the image doesn't make sense, so they won't try again.

AI ONLINE

Online security is one area in which AI is starting to have a big impact on everyday life. Security technology is always trying to stay one step ahead of online crime, and to protect us in our homes and workplaces.

ANTIVIRUS AI

One of the biggest risks to computer users is **malware**, such as viruses. If this type of software gets into a computer system, it 'copies' and attaches itself to different files. A virus can corrupt or destroy data. It can also give criminals access to information stored on the computer.

Antivirus software can detect patterns that indicate if a file has been infected. But traditional software can only identify patterns its programmers already know about. Intelligent antivirus software could be trained to learn from existing patterns. It may then be able to adapt that knowledge to recognise and stop new viruses.

CAPTCHA

Have you ever had to fill in a CAPTCHA before a website will let you in? CAPTCHA are tests that humans can complete but current computer technology can't. The tests often involve recognising letters and numbers in different positions or with lines over them. They are designed to stop **bots** accessing websites.

i'm a captcha!

i'm not a robot

CAPTCHA
Privacy · Terms

Eps10 vector

Type the two words:

CAPTCHA
Privacy · Terms

CAPTCHA stands for **C**ompletely **A**utomated **P**ublic **T**uring test to tell **C**omputers and **H**umans **A**part.

SPOTTING SPAM

Email services such as Gmail use AI to filter emails and identify unwanted ones. By looking at the sender and the content, they can sort emails into categories including spam. Google even uses an amazing artificial neural network to identify and block spam that looks like real emails.

WHAT IF...? Security is a big concern in today's digital world, and AI is helping to make our online actions more secure. But what might happen if AI technology gets into the wrong hands? Could it be used for criminal activity? Should that stop us from developing it?

Every time you fill in a CAPTCHA or RECAPTCHA code, you're helping to improve Google's artificial intelligence. The information you type in, based on the words and photographs you see, 'trains' the AI. For example, by clicking on all the grid squares with a car in, you're helping the software get better at identifying cars.

AI
IN ACTION

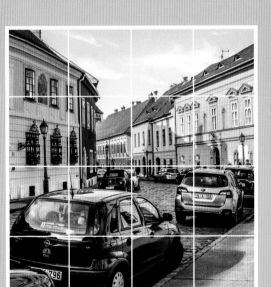

THE AI EFFECT

The definition of AI is always changing. The things we considered 'intelligent' ten years ago are so widely used now that they're no longer regarded as AI. Experts call this 'the AI effect'. So, what are the latest definitions of AI? And what might they be in the future?

FACIAL ID

Artificial intelligence that can recognise people's faces is one of the fastest-developing areas of AI. And it's not just about being able to organise your photos online. Soon, credit card information and driving licences may be linked to your face, so you won't need to carry identification around with you!

What is intelligence? These days, many people define 'intelligence' as anything a human can do that a machine can't. So, it's no surprise that what we think of as AI is always changing!

CHATBOTS – THE NEXT GENERATION

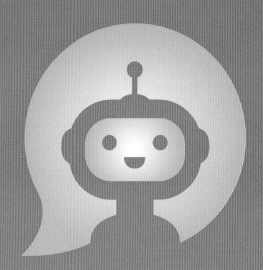

It's already difficult to know whether some online interactions are with a human or a chatbot. In the future, chatbots may not only be able to work out what you need, they may also be able to understand how you're feeling. Experts are working on a type of 'digital **empathy**' to make chatbots even more human-like.

THE FUTURE IN THE PAST

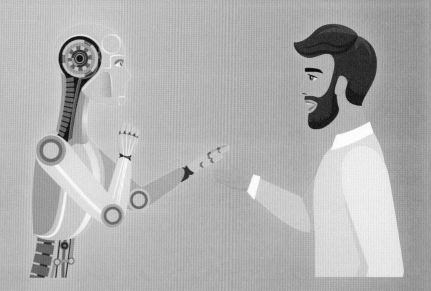

Scientists first began discussing artificial intelligence in the first half of the twentieth century. Back then, their goal was to create a general intelligence – one that could solve lots of different problems. But they ended up setting aside this huge task and focusing on AI that tackled individual problems. Today, however, AI experts are dusting off that original aim and thinking big once more.

With all the advances in AI over the past 50 years, perhaps truly intelligent machines may soon be science fact rather than science fiction.

WHAT IF...? What if intelligent computers develop less desirable human characteristics? For example, they might learn to be **biased** about certain things. Should we accept that this is part of the process of creating a truly human-like machine? Or should we try to make them 'perfect'? Who should decide what 'perfect' really means?

GLOSSARY

algorithm – a set of steps that tell a computer what to do in order to solve a problem or perform a task

bias – prejudice for or against someone or something, often in a way that is considered to be unfair

binary code – a coding system that uses only the numbers 0 and 1 in different combinations

bot – a computer program that can interact with systems or users on the internet

chatbot – a computer program designed to be able to hold human-like conversations

cognitive scientist – a scientist who specialises in understanding how thought processes work

computer science – the science of how computers work and how information is managed, transformed and encoded in computer systems

empathy – the ability to understand and share someone else's feelings

ethical – relating to whether things are right or wrong

fundamental operator – a basic symbol or word that represents an action or operation that a computer makes

hardware – the physical parts of a computer, such as the screen, keyboard and mouse

instinct – knowing something or behaving automatically, without learning or thinking about it

intuition – the ability to understand something by instinct rather than reasoning

malware – malicious software, designed to steal or destroy information on a computer

neural networks – algorithms that recognise patterns and interpret data in a similar way to how the human brain works

neuron – a nerve cell that carries messages around the body and to the brain in the form of electrical impulses

neuroscience – the study of how the brain and nervous system are connected and work in the human body

node – a data point on a plotted route, which contains information such as a value or condition; nodes can be connected to other nodes

pixel – a unit of light on a computer screen that forms part of an image

psychology – the study of the human mind and human behaviour

reasoning – working through information logically to reach the right answer

recall – the process of retrieving information from the memory

software – the programs that give computers the instructions they need to work

FIND OUT MORE

BOOKS

Machine Learning (Explore AI) by Sonya Newland (Wayland, 2021)

AI (The Tech Head Guide) by William Potter (Wayland, 2020)

Computers (The Tech Head Guide) by William Potter (Wayland, 2020)

WEBSITES

www.bbc.co.uk/teach/alan-turing-creator-of-modern-computing/zhwp7nb

Find out all about computer genius Alan Turing.

www.bbc.co.uk/newsround/49274918

Discover more about what AI is and what it does.

INDEX

BRAINY COMPUTERS

INTELLIGENT ROBOTS

SMART DEVICES

MACHINE LEARNING